RUTH FIRST NEVER BACKED DOWN

Ruth First was my friend. She was a brilliant journalist, writer, and university professor who was accepted into the ranks of the Black liberation struggle against apartheid. Today she is honored as one of the world's great fighters for racial justice, gender equity, and democracy. I'm glad Danielle is sharing Ruth's story with young readers.

—JUSTICE ALBIE SACHS

In memory of my aunt, Dr. Brenda Leibowitz, for her dedication to equality in education. And to all the human rights activists who never backed down.

—D.J.

KAR-BEN PUBLISHING®
An imprint of Lerner Publishing Group, Inc.
241 First Avenue North
Minneapolis, MN 55401 USA
Website address: www.karben.com

Main body text set in Tw Cen MT Std Medium.
Typeface provided by Monotype Typography.

Library of Congress Cataloging-in-Publication Data

Names: Joseph, Danielle, author. | Utomo, Gabhor, illustrator.
Title: Ruth First never backed down / Danielle Joseph ; illustrated by Gabhor Utomo.
Description: Minneapolis, MN : Kar-Ben Publishing, [2023] | Audience: Ages 4–8 | Audience: Grades K–1 | Summary: "Ruth First was born in South Africa, where her Jewish family fled from the danger in Europe during WWII. Committed to speaking out against apartheid, she did so all her life, never backing down"— Provided by publisher.
Identifiers: LCCN 2022040485 (print) | LCCN 2022040486 (ebook) | ISBN 9781728460284 (lib. bdg.) | ISBN 9781728495545 (eb pdf)
Subjects: LCSH: First, Ruth, 1925-1982—Juvenile literature. | Women anti-apartheid activists—South Africa—Biography—Juvenile literature. | Anti-apartheid activists—South Africa—Biography—Juvenile literature. | Women political prisoners—South Africa—Biography—Juvenile literature. | Political prisoners—South Africa—Biography—Juvenile literature. | Women journalists—South Africa—Biography—Juvenile literature. | Journalists—South Africa—Biography—Juvenile literature. | South Africa—Race relations—History—20th century—Juvenile literature.
Classification: LCC DT1927.F57 J67 2023 (print) | LCC DT1927.F57 (ebook) | DDC 305.800968/09045 [B]—dc23/eng/20220826

LC record available at https://lccn.loc.gov/2022040485
LC ebook record available at https://lccn.loc.gov/2022040486

Manufactured in the United States of America
1-51490-50375-12/6/2022

RUTH FIRST
NEVER BACKED DOWN

DANIELLE JOSEPH

illustrated by **GABHOR UTOMO**

KAR-BEN
PUBLISHING

Mother Africa loves all her children.

With open arms, she welcomes immigrants fleeing violence.

Ruth First felt Mother Africa's warmth early on. Her Jewish grandparents had faced dangers and injustices in Eastern Europe.

They escaped by boat to the country of South Africa, where Ruth's parents grew up in safety. Ruth was born there.

But South Africa had a system called apartheid that
separated Black people from white people. Black
people had far fewer rights than white people.

Ruth's parents knew this was wrong. They held meetings in their house where they spoke out against anti-Black racism.

Ruth saw how many people looked the other way instead of fighting injustice. She wanted to take action. As a young teen, she started a book club with her friends. They met in secret to discuss books about inequality.

In high school, Ruth knew she had to do more. It wasn't enough to talk about injustice privately with people who already agreed with her. She needed to speak out in public, to try to change other people's minds about apartheid.

She grabbed a megaphone, charged up the steps of City Hall, and cried out for freedom for all South Africans.

Mother Africa heard her cries and said, *Use your voice to fight this injustice.*

In college, Ruth wrote stories for the school newspaper. She reported on how South African police officers targeted Black people—treating them unfairly and often hurting or killing them.

Sometimes, people gathered to publicly protest these injustices. The police tried to shut down protests and injured many protesters.

During one protest, Ruth jumped in front of police officers to snap a photograph of them. Ruth could've been hurt, but she did not back down. She was out to tell the truth.

During her studies, she met other activists: Eduardo Mondlane, Fatima Meer, Ismail Meer . . . And then there was a law student who had given up the chance to become a village chief to join the anti-apartheid movement. His name was Nelson Mandela. Together the group fought to tear down the racist laws.

In the dark of the night, armed with a flashlight and a camera, Ruth dug deep as an investigative journalist. She exposed the terrible working conditions that Black miners and farmers faced. And she helped spread the ideas of Black activists, whose work was being ignored by many other journalists.

The government worked to silence the freedom fighters. New laws forbade any resistance to apartheid. Ruth was no longer allowed to work as a journalist. The newspaper she edited was banned, but she kept working on it illegally. She and her friends met in secret.

One night, the police raided Ruth's house. Behind a bookcase, they found the illegal newspaper that she edited and threw her in prison. She was the first white woman to be arrested under the new law against anti-apartheid activities.

Ruth was held in solitary confinement.
She was allowed no books. No paper.
No contact with the outside world.

The government wanted her to name the
other people who were working against
apartheid. Ruth refused to betray her
friends. She remained silent.

The harsh conditions
nearly destroyed her.

But Mother Africa picked her up and said,
Use your voice to keep on fighting.

Ruth was released from prison but forced to leave the country.

Ruth's love for Mother Africa ran as deep as the ocean. She could taste the salt of Mother Africa's tears.

Great Britain became Ruth's new home. There, she wrote articles and books about the horrors of apartheid. She made a movie about her experiences and gave speeches detailing the extreme racism she'd witnessed. She would not back down.

After thirteen years, Ruth returned to Mother Africa's embrace. Still not allowed back in South Africa, she settled in Mozambique.

She taught at Eduardo Mondlane University and continued to fight for equality. She traveled all over the continent, speaking up about injustice wherever she went.

But five years later, on August 17, 1982, Ruth First was stolen from Mother Africa. She was targeted by the South African government. She lost her life because she was a voice of freedom.

Ruth will always be a part of Mother Africa's tapestry, woven into her fabric.

It was because of voices like Ruth's that the apartheid system finally ended in the 1990s. Nelson Mandela said, "Her life and her death remain a beacon to all who love liberty."

Timeline

1905: Black people are banned from voting in South Africa.

1910–1936: The South African government passes a series of laws taking more rights away from Black people.

1912: The African National Congress (ANC), a political party focused on human rights for all South Africans, is founded.

1925: Ruth First is born in Johannesburg, South Africa.

1946: Ruth graduates from the University of the Witwatersrand with a bachelor's degree in social studies. She begins working as a journalist.

1948: The South African government passes laws to make apartheid the official national policy.

1949: Ruth marries Joe Slovo, a lawyer, writer, and anti-apartheid activist.

1953: Ruth joins the Congress Alliance, a political group resisting apartheid.

1956: Ruth, Joe, and other members of the Congress Alliance are arrested and charged with high treason. Ruth and Joe are cleared of the charges, but others are imprisoned, executed, or driven out of the country.

1963: Ruth is arrested and imprisoned for anti-apartheid activism.

1964: After her release from prison, Ruth leaves South Africa and moves to Great Britain with Joe and their three daughters, Shawn, Gillian, and Robyn.

1965: Ruth publishes her book *117 Days*, which describes her experiences in prison.

1966: Ruth writes and stars in the BBC film *Ninety Days* about her time in detention.

1977: Ruth moves to Mozambique and becomes the director of research for the Center for African Studies at Eduardo Mondlane University.

1982: Ruth is killed instantly by a bomb sent by the South African Security Police.

1990: The South African government and the ANC begin negotiations to end apartheid.

1994: For the first time, Black people in South Africa are allowed to vote in a national election. Nelson Mandela is elected president of South Africa, ending the apartheid era.

Other Leaders in the Anti-Apartheid Movement

Frances Baard (1909–1997) was a South African human rights and workers' rights activist. She helped form the ANC Women's League and helped lead the Federation of South African Women.

Nelson Mandela (1918–2013) was a South African activist. He cofounded the ANC Youth League and was jailed in 1962 for opposing the South African government. Released from prison in 1990, he received the Nobel Peace Prize for helping to end apartheid. In 1994, Mandela became the first Black president of South Africa.

Fatima Meer (1928–2010) was a South African professor, human rights activist, and author. She was a founding member of the Federation of South African Women. In 1951 and 1952, she helped launch the Defiance Campaign against Unjust Laws, a series of powerful political demonstrations.

Ismail Meer (1918–2000) was a South African lawyer, writer, and activist. He was the husband of freedom fighter Fatima Meer.

Eduardo Mondlane (1920–1969) was a revolutionary leader, political activist, and scholar born in Mozambique. He was president of the Mozambique Liberation Front. In 1969, he was killed by a letter bomb in Tanzania. In 1976, the University of Lourenço Marques in Mozambique was renamed Eduardo Mondlane University.

Lillian Ngoyi (1911–1980) was a South African nurse, seamstress, and anti-apartheid activist. She was elected president of the ANC Women's League in 1953. She also helped to form and lead the Federation of South African Women. In 1956 she was the first woman elected to the ANC's executive committee. She was arrested in 1956 and confined to house arrest for the rest of her life.

Albie Sachs (b. 1935) is a South African human rights activist, lawyer, and author. Targeted by the South African government, he was the victim of a car bomb and lost his right arm and his eyesight in one eye during his fight against apartheid. He helped write South Africa's new constitution in the 1990s and served as a justice on the country's highest court for fifteen years.

Walter Sisulu (1912–2003) was a South African freedom fighter and cofounder of the ANC Youth League. He was imprisoned for more than twenty-five years alongside Nelson Mandela and later became deputy president of the ANC.

Joe Slovo (1926–1995) was born in Lithuania and moved to South Africa as a child. He was a lawyer and freedom fighter and married Ruth First in 1949. He was a leader of the military wing of the ANC. He served as South Africa's minister of housing in 1994.

Desmond Tutu (1931–2021) was a South African human rights activist and Nobel Peace Prize winner. He was the first Black African to become an Anglican bishop in Johannesburg and later archbishop in Cape Town. He was chairman of the Truth and Reconciliation Commission, a court set up in the 1990s to investigate human rights violations that had been committed during apartheid.

About the Author

Danielle Joseph was born in Cape Town, South Africa. The author of several young adult novels and picture books, she lives in Maryland with her husband, three kids, and a dog named Ringo. When not writing, she can be found swimming, listening to music, and chasing after her dog.

About the Illustrator

Gabhor Utomo was born and raised in Indonesia. He received his degree from the Academy of Art University in San Francisco. He lives with his wife and twin daughters in Portland, Oregon.